# chardonnay

DISCOVERING EXPLORING ENJOYING

# chardonnay

DISCOVERING EXPLORING ENJOYING

CHRIS LOSH

RYLAND
PETERS
& SMALL

LONDON  NEW YORK

**Designer** Pamela Daniels
**Senior Editor** Clare Double
**Picture Research** Emily Westlake
**Production** Deborah Wehner
**Art Director** Gabriella Le Grazie
**Publishing Director** Alison Starling

10 9 8 7 6 5 4 3 2 1

Printed and bound in China
First published in the United States in 2004
by Ryland Peters & Small, Inc.
519 Broadway, 5th Floor
New York NY 10012
www.rylandpeters.com

Text © Chris Losh 2004
Design and commissioned photography
© Ryland Peters & Small 2004

Library of Congress Cataloging-in-Publication Data

Losh, Chris.
  Chardonnay : discovering exploring enjoying / Chris Losh.
    p. cm.
  Includes index.
  ISBN 1-84172-699-0
  1. Chardonnay (Wine) I. Title.
  TP548.L685 2004
  641.2'222--dc22

                                    2004003831

# contents

Imagine that you are a megalomaniac scientist, creating a grape to take over the world. What criteria might you want in your Franken-wine's monster?

First off, you'd want a grape capable of making good cheap wines and top-class expensive ones; that could be drunk with food or in front of the TV; and was versatile enough to make everything from bone-dry sparklers to super-sweet dessert wines. Stylistically, you'd want it to range from lean, lemony, and steely to big, tropical, and buttery. Finally, you'd need an exotic name that was still easy to remember, and pronounceable the world over. And then you'd realize that you were too late and somebody got there before you with Chardonnay.

The name on millions of bottles around the world, it's become the nearest thing to a global wine brand name—a guarantee of reliability. But what makes Chardonnay so special, how does its flavor change around the world, and how can you get the most out of it? Read on…

# DISCOVERING

# flavor

*If the Chardonnay grape were a person,*
*you'd want it to be your best friend.*

Sure, there are other grape varieties with stronger personalities—the intellectual Riesling, the brooding and complicated Nebbiolo, the tortured genius of Pinot Noir.

But Chardonnay just wants to have fun. It's tolerant, cheerful, and good-natured, bending over backwards to make life easier for the people who grow it, the people who make wine with it—and, yes, the people who drink it. It's the ultimate good-time grape.

Which is one of the reasons that it's everywhere you look. Not just on supermarket shelves, restaurant wine lists, and in fine-wine merchants—but all around the world as well. While some vines are finicky and temperamental, unable to turn out

good fruit unless everything from soil to aspect to rainfall to sunshine is spot on, Chardonnay is too laidback to care over-much.

While there are obviously some places that suit it better than others (the chalk and limestone soils of Burgundy being a case in point), Chardonnay is able to make eminently drinkable wine in the most diverse locations imaginable.

It does OK in the irrigated desert of the Australian Riverland and in the chilly hills of northern France, in the relentless sun of Chile's Rapel Valley and the swirling fogs of southern California. From the shores of the Great Lakes to the Cape of Good Hope, Chardonnay is a grape that travels with a smile. And if it turns up its roots in disgust at a location, then it's probably a site that isn't fit for growing anything.

Of all of the top grape varieties, Chardonnay is probably the easiest to grow. Give it some sun and a

*Chardonnay is a grape*
*that travels with a smile.*

Give it some sun and a bit
of water, and Chardonnay will turn out
juicily ripe grapes, even if a
location is really too hot or too cold.

bit of water, and it will turn out juicily ripe grapes,
even if a location is really too hot or too cold.

It's ridiculously hardy. In the vineyard the only
two major worries with Chardonnay are that its
early budding makes it vulnerable to spring frosts,
while if there's too much rain and the grapes swell,
its thin skins can split.

The third problem with Chardonnay is, as you
might expect for such a positive grape variety, that
it errs on the side of overenthusiasm. Left to its own
devices, the vine will churn out stacks and stacks of
grapes, and huge great bushy canopies of leaves—
neither of which does anything for quality.

More conscientious growers work hard at limiting the vine's productivity. But such vigorousness helps to explain why, for less scrupulous producers in search of quantity rather than quality, Chardonnay is often the grape of choice. If you're looking for high yields of unremarkable but drinkable plonk, there's no better grape.

Some in the wine world worry about its ubiquity, fearing that we might drown in a sea of easy-drinking, made-by-numbers Chardonnay. But it's hard to give much credence to the ABC (Anything But Chardonnay) brigade, because even mile-a-minute Chardonnays are rarely actually bad. Boring, yes; characterless, for sure; but still highly drinkable. A lot of the wines might be nothing to write home about, but the reliability of your average Chardonnay is understandably appealing to consumers faced with hundreds of bottles in a wine store.

The grape delivers at pretty much any price, with a catalog of consistency and flexibility that puts every other grape variety—red or white—to shame. Chardonnay deserves its success.

## MODERN ROMANCE

Perhaps another reason for our love affair with Chardonnay is the way it fits in with our impatient here-and-now lifestyles. OK, the best wines (usually Burgundies) should be aged for ten or even 20 plus years, and some top wines from the New World benefit from five to ten years in bottle. But over 95 percent of all Chardonnays are designed to be drunk as soon as they're bought, and won't improve significantly with time.

They might just as well come with a big Alice-in-Wonderland label attached saying, "Drink Me."

The grape delivers at pretty much any price, with a catalog of consistency and flexibility that puts every other grape variety—red or white—to shame.

# Unlike most white grapes, Chardonnay loves oak.

So, what does Chardonnay actually taste like? Well, oddly enough, not all that much in its pure state, which is both the grape's big blessing and also, in the wrong hands, its curse. One of the more neutral-flavored grapes, Chardonnay is often characterized by a soft melony aroma. What this offers, though, is a clean slate, on which both the place where it's grown and the winemaker can leave their marks.

Chardonnay changes style significantly from location to location, expressing what the French call the vineyard's "terroir." Compare lean, minerally Chablis and the fat, tropical flavors from the Rapel Valley, for instance. The same grape gives very different wines.

This same neutrality makes it something of a blank canvas for winemakers, too, who can tweak and twiddle the flavors to get a final product that they like. This has both its good and its bad points.

On the one hand, it can mean highly drinkable wine from unexciting raw material. On the other, it can lead to charges of sameness—that all the wines have been molded to fit an internationally acceptable profile, rather than being allowed to express their site's character.

Winemakers have dozens of character-changing techniques at their disposal. They can add acidity to overripe wines, soften acidity with malolactic fermentation (making crisp acidity into softer, lactic acid), or leave it as it is. They can leave the wine on the lees to add a rich, creamy character, or go for a more citrussy style. They can ferment it cold in stainless steel for a fresher, fruitier taste, or in oak barrels for less up-front fruit and more complexity and depth. Or they can do various percentages of wines in each process and put it all together at the end like a giant vinous jigsaw puzzle.

Of all these processes, the use (or not) of wood is arguably the most important. Unlike most white grapes, Chardonnay loves oak. Either fermenting the wine in oak barrels or leaving it to age in them for a while gives it a spicy, toasty, vanilla flavor, which fits well with the grape's round, generous character and gives a real mouth-filler in your glass.

Winemakers need to be careful, though. Add too much wood, and the result is an out-of-balance wine where the oak dominates and all freshness is lost. This was particularly common in the early 1990s—and especially with Australian and California Chardonnays, some of which you practically had to cut with a saw before drinking.

But winemakers have learned, and it's no exaggeration to say that there's a real cross-pollination of ideas going on. Chileans have learned from Australians, who have learned from Californians, who have lifted some techniques used in Burgundy's Côte d'Or. This has led to a certain confusion—picking a wine's provenance in a blind tasting can be tough now, even for the people who made them! But it's also led to more good wine, and that, surely, is what it's all about.

Chardonnay's advance doesn't look like grinding to a halt any time soon.

### PINOT PEDIGREE

Oddly enough for such a famous grape, until recently no one was exactly sure where Chardonnay came from. There were suggestions that the grape came originally from the Middle East, or that it arrived in France from Cyprus.

Now, though, DNA testing has revealed that it is a cross of two French varieties: the red star of Burgundy, Pinot Noir, and the white also-ran Gouais Blanc. They must be delighted with how their baby has turned out!

Wine is a living product. That's what makes it so interesting. If you leave it in a bottle for a few years, it changes character. If you buy the same wine from the same producer, but two years apart, it will taste different. And if you buy two wines from the same year, but different vineyards, they will have their own characteristics as well. That is the effect of terroir—the influence that local climate and soils have on a wine's flavor. It's at its most pronounced in Burgundy, where distances of a few yards can cause big differences in flavor, but it applies all around the world. And Chardonnay, probably more than any other grape, has literally put down roots wherever grapes are grown, from China to Chile and England to Oz.

So let's embark on a global tour to see just how the world's favorite white grape behaves in the main places where it's grown.

# EXPLORING

# burgundy

is Chardonnay's homeland. It's the place that gives the most complex and inspiring expressions of the grape anywhere in the world, the base from which Chardonnay has headed out on its pilgrimage across vineyards from California to Cape Town.

So how is it that the same grape that makes cheap and cheerful wines in one place can take on such extraordinary complexity in the hands of a committed Burgundian? Apart from obvious factors such as lower yields and good winemaking, the answer is terroir—that untranslatable French word that means a combination of soil, weather, and microclimate.

By one of those happy accidents of geography, parts of Burgundy are simply climatically and geologically perfect for making great Chardonnay. Not, by the way, that all Burgundy is great. Far from it. Too much of it is under-flavored and overpriced, trading on the region's reputation as a whole. But, when things do come together in the region, the rest of the world can only watch in envy. Other places can mimic Burgundy's winemaking techniques, but it's impossible for them to imitate her terroir.

Wine has been made in Burgundy since Roman times—and probably long before that. It's a long, thin region, but it's not particularly big, and its production compared to, say, Bordeaux is relatively small. It's less grand, too. While Bordeaux is known for its imposing châteaux, Burgundy retains a more downhome feel; more denim overalls than tweed suit.

Not, alas, that this makes it any more approachable. Burgundy might not be enormous, but it's very fragmented, with hundreds of appellations and thousands of growers. Even small vineyard sites are split up among dozens of growers, all of whom have different ideas on what constitutes good winemaking. Burgundy is many things, but simple isn't one of them.

Let's start by splitting it into three parts. Chablis is the farthest north (see pages 20–21), standing slightly apart from the rest of the north–south streak of vineyards. The Côte d'Or is at the heart of the region, and home to its most famous names. Then to the south are the vineyards of the Côte Chalonnaise and the Mâconnais (see page 22).

If Burgundy in general is Chardonnay's homeland, then the Côte d'Or is its armchair in front of the fire. It's where the grape feels most comfortable; home of vineyard names that have passed into legend.

Terroir—that untranslatable French word that means a combination of soil, weather, and microclimate.

This is a region that is all about minutiae: where wines from a vineyard on one side of a stone wall taste different from those on the other.

"Côte d'Or" means "golden slope," so called because of the brilliant swath of yellows, oranges, and reds that characterizes the vineyards in the fall. It's split into two regions, with the wine capital, Beaune, more or less in the middle. The northern part, the Côte de Nuits, is largely red-wine country, home to stellar Pinot Noir vineyards. Chardonnay is planted here, but generally speaking the soils are too heavy and claylike for it, and the grape prefers to be farther south on the slopes of the Côte de Beaune, which are 75 percent white.

So why the difference? Ask the locals and they will say three things are the key to great white Burgundy: limestone, limestone, and limestone. There's a big ridge of the stuff across the Côte de Beaune—and Chardonnay loves it.

Not that it's easy for the grape. The Côte de Beaune may be south of Chablis, but it's still quite a way north and close to the limit where it's possible to ripen Chardonnay fully. In a cloudy or rainy year, most of the wines are rarely anything to write home about. Yet it's the fact that Burgundy is so close to not being able to make Chardonnay work that is one of the keys to its success. The grapes take longer to ripen here than in warmer places, which gives them more time to develop their flavors. Plus, since it cools off at night, they can retain a good, fresh acidity. And when Burgundy gets it right, it gets it spectacularly right.

So what do Chardonnay grapes taste like? Well, it's impossible to generalize. Flavors can go from lighter apples, melons, and lemons to extraordinarily intense aromas of nuts, mangoes, quince, honeysuckle, figs, honey... I could go on.

This is a region that is all about minutiae: where tiny changes in exposure or soil content make big differences to the character of the wine; where wines from a vineyard on one side of a stone wall taste different from those on the other.

It's this influence of terroir that makes Burgundy so complicated—and also so fascinating. The Burgundians have tried to help us out with a whole hierarchy of appellations, from Grand Cru at the top through Premier Cru, more general village appellations, and finally straight Burgundy, which can come from anywhere in the region.

The trouble is that the soils are so complicated and the classifications so numerous that it's easy to get confused. Not only that, but since each classified vineyard is home to many different growers, quality can vary hugely.

Puligny-Montrachet, for instance, might be one of the greatest wine regions in the world, but not all of the growers with vines there make great wine. There is some fabulous wine in the Côte d'Or, but to find it you need to have the right site and the right producer—plus, in all probability, the right vintage. Oh, and deep pockets...

No one ever said it was easy, and yet it's still somehow worth it. Few winemakers anywhere would argue with the statement that good white Burgundy is the greatest expression of Chardonnay in the world. Made well, it's so much more than just another Chardonnay. It's an expression of a time and a place; a winemaker's vision captured in a bottle. And if that's not worth a bit of extra effort, then I don't know what is.

## top areas

CHASSAGNE-MONTRACHET

MEURSAULT

PULIGNY-MONTRACHET

## grand cru sites

BÂTARD-MONTRACHET

CHEVALIER MONTRACHET

CORTON-CHARLEMAGNE

LE MONTRACHET

## producers to watch

## burgundy

COCHE-DURY

JOSEPH DROUHIN

LOUIS JADOT

HENRI JAYER

DOMINIQUE LAFON

LOUIS LATOUR

DOMAINE LEFLAIVE

Ask the locals and they will say three things are the key to great white Burgundy: limestone, limestone, and limestone.

Genuine Chablis comes from a small region southwest of Paris, and is made only with Chardonnay.

## CHABLIS

With the exceptions of Champagne, which uses it for fizz, and Canada, where the grape remains something of a rarity, Chablis is the most northerly Chardonnay-growing region in the world. It's also one of the best known — but be careful. Outside Europe, not all of the bottles bearing the name Chablis have anything to do with this northern outpost of Burgundy. Many New World countries have used the name as shorthand for home-produced "white wine" — and qualitatively and stylistically, they are a different animal.

Genuine Chablis comes only from a small region about 125 miles (200 km) southwest of Paris, and is made only with Chardonnay. Although it's still officially part of Burgundy, Chablis is actually nearer to Champagne. A long way north, it's right on the limit of where it's possible to ripen the grape enough to make table wine, and in poor years you'll need to pick your wines with care. Dilute, underripe Chablis is not a pleasant experience, and it's not as uncommon as it should be.

In such a marginal climate, making a living from grapes can be a hair-raising process for the growers. Chardonnay buds early, and spring frosts in chilly old Chablis are a real problem. Forty years ago, growers deserted the region in their droves, fed up with having their crop decimated by springtime cold snaps. In recent years, though, frost protection methods have improved out of sight, and the vineyards have grown significantly as a result.

The best vineyards (the Grands Crus) are north of the town on steep, southwest-facing slopes. This allows the vines to catch all the precious afternoon and evening sun, giving wines with greater ripeness than those from less favorable sites. In good years, these seven Grands Crus can produce some truly sublime wines, all with very different characters.

Good Chablis is typified by a kind of taut leanness. The wines are toned and stony, with flashes of citrus fruit and flowers and what the French call "nervosité"—a kind of inner tension. They are, in short, a million miles away from the fatter, more luscious, tropical versions from many New World producers.

While this might make them unpalatable to some, it gives them one great plus point: longevity. Grand Cru wines need to be aged a minimum of ten years before they start to give their best, and will happily go for 20 years, while the best Premiers Crus will easily last a decade. The standard Chablis and Petit Chablis wines are best drunk young, and, in off-vintages, probably not at all.

Traditional Chablis would typically not have seen any wood influence, giving a clean, steely wine, but plenty of producers now are playing around with oak barrels. This lessens differences in flavor between the different crus, but it does give rather rounder wines and helps them to age.

The region's producers can't agree on whether this increased use of wood is a good thing or not, but what is undeniably true is that Chablis from a good producer, a good site, and a good vintage remains one of the bargains of the white-wine world.

## producers to watch
## chablis

| | |
|---|---|
| DOMAINE DES MALANDES | LAROCHE |
| JEAN-PAUL DROIN | J. MOREAU ET FILS |
| JOSEPH DROUHIN | FRANÇOIS ET JEAN-MARIE |
| ALAIN GEOFFROY | RAVENEAU |

## chablis' seven grand cru sites

LES BLANCHOTS

LES BOUGROS

LES CLOS

LES GRENOUILLES

LES PREUSES

VALMUR

VAUDÉSIR

## SOUTHERN BURGUNDY

If you've only ever bought one bottle of white Burgundy, chances are it came from the south. When the famous names of the Côte de Beaune finish, the Côte Chalonnaise and the Mâconnais take over. Generally speaking, wines here are less intense than those of their big brother to the north; if you will, more Chardonnaylike and less Burgundian.

The Côte Chalonnaise, sandwiched between the Côte d'Or to the north and Mâcon to the south, has been a forgotten region for Burgundy. It has less protection from mountains than its northern neighbor, and some of the vineyards are higher, so grapes don't get so intensely ripe. The result is lighter, chalkier wines, many of which used to make a base for local sparkling wines. Those from the Rully area are probably the leanest and most elegant (a good bet in hotter years, when other places get overripe). Those from Montagny are fuller, with more honeyed flavors, and good value for money.

The Mâconnais is Burgundy's Chardonnay engine room. This area makes three times as much wine from the grape as the rest of Burgundy put together. It's warmer and flatter than the Chalonnais and the Côte d'Or and, with more clay and less of the crucial limestone, tends to give a kind of "Burgundy-lite" flavor. Few of the wines spend time in oak barrels, and the flavors are juicily approachable melons and apples.

Historically, most growers here sold their wines to cooperatives, which blended the whole lot together, but more and more of them are starting to realize the region's potential and make more personalized wines. Not, some might say, before time.

There is one shining exception of regional character and quality within the Mâconnais, however: Pouilly-Fuissé, a series of swirling limestone hills at Burgundy's southernmost tip. South of here the limestone runs out—as did the lives of many animals in the Stone Age. Hunters killed them by the hi-tech method of chasing them off the chalky cliffs. The wines are a bit friendlier: with more heat and those famous alkaline, Chardonnay-friendly soils, they can have real depth and an exotic richness.

This being Burgundy, of course, quality varies wildly, but a string of famous names have set up here over the last ten years and they're setting standards for others to match.

### wineries to watch
### southern burgundy

JOSEPH DROUHIN

DOMAINE J.-A. FERRET

LOUIS JADOT

HENRI LAFARGE

LOUIS LATOUR

OLIVIER MERLIN

VERGET

Did you know that Chardonnay is one of the principal grapes used in champagne? Probably not. Few people realize that the variety is such a major part of the world's most famous fizz (comprising over a quarter of all the grapes in the Champagne region), because it doesn't appear on the label.

That's because the rules of the region's governing body don't allow it, but in any case not many champagnes are made with one single grape variety. It does happen—anything labeled "blanc de blancs," for instance, will be 100 percent Chardonnay—but they're something of a minority. Most of the region's wines are a blend of different grapes (red grapes Pinot Noir and Pinot Meunier are the other two). In fact, it is the ability to blend the different grapes with the characteristics offered by different vineyards to make a consistent house style that is the big skill of a champagne house's maître de chai. And it really is a skill. Some of the finished blends are made up of over 100 wines.

# champagne

The joy of this most majestic of drinks is that the components create so much more than the sum of their parts.

Most of the Chardonnay in Champagne is grown on the east-facing slopes of the Côte des Blancs—a sweep of chalky hills running south of the town of Epernay. We already know how much Chardonnay loves chalk, but why east-facing? Surely there's more sun to be had facing south or west?

Well, maybe there is. But sun isn't the problem in Champagne—there's plenty of that. However, there's also plenty of wind, and this far north (don't forget we're level with Paris here) it really keeps the temperatures down. On the eastern slopes the vines are protected from the predominant westerly winds, allowing them to ripen.

Not that most of them ever do attain "proper" maturity. Nibble on a Champagne grape straight from the vine and your face will screw up as though you're eating a lemon. These grapes are much lower in sugar and flavor and much higher in acidity than their counterparts in still-wine regions.

And the Champenois love it that way. It is this acidity that will provide the wines with their "backbone" and allow them to age for years. Without it, champers would be dull, lifeless, and as elegant as a pair of grape picker's dungarees.

Champagne starts out as a still wine. Made from those high-acid, barely ripe grapes, it's typically fresh, elegant, low in alcohol and, frankly, not very exciting. At this stage, winemakers look for more delicate flavors of flowers, nuts, and a zip of citrus rather than real high-octane fruit flavors.

But next comes the magic. Wineries add a shot of wine, sugar, and yeast, and the Mr. Unremarkable wine starts a second fermentation in the bottle. That's where the bubbles and the "normal" alcohol level come from. More complex flavors come with time, as the young fizz is left to mature in the bottle.

Chardonnay typically brings a creamy, lemony note to a bottle of champagne, but part of the joy of this most majestic of drinks is that, when all the different components are added together, they manage to combine to create so much more than the sum of their parts. Santé!

## famous all-chardonnay champagnes

JACQUESSON BLANC DE BLANCS
  GRAND CRU VINTAGE
KRUG CLOS DU MESNIL
RUINART BLANC DE BLANCS VINTAGE

While there's no question that the majority of Chardonnay in France (three-quarters of it, in fact) is accounted for by plantings in Burgundy and Champagne, the grape has settled in elsewhere, too.

# rest of france

Perhaps its least-known location is in the far east of the country, in the mountains of Jura near the Swiss border. Since it's just east of Burgundy, it's perhaps not surprising to find the grape here, but production is small. One for the connoisseurs.

Swinging across the country to the Loire Valley as far as Anjou, you'll find the grape again. Anjou used to be rosé territory, but changes in our drinking habits have seen a shift of emphasis. And, since it's too cool this far north and close to the coast to get decent red grapes to ripen, that means white grapes.

All of which is good news for Chardonnay, and it is now permitted to add the grape to the local Chenin Blanc. It's also helping to make what can be rather austere wines rounder and more accessible.

Farther east in Saumur, Chardonnay (grown on similarly chalky soils to Champagne) can be added to the region's sparkling wines, up to a maximum of 20 percent. That maximum is instructive. Although Chardonnay is on the up in the Loire, it remains very much an also-ran—an additional extra rather than the raison (or should that be raisin) d'être.

While French Chardonnay is at its classiest in cooler, northern areas, it's also gaining ground in the sunshine of the Mediterranean—and chances are that any non-Burgundian French Chardonnays you've tasted will have come from here.

More and more producers are discovering that the Languedoc is a good place to make decent, well-priced wines. And the regulations of the Vin de Pays d'Oc mean it's possible to make 100 percent Chardonnay—and to label it as such, which makes it easier for potential customers to understand. These wines are fruit-forward and well-made rather than exciting, but they've proved they can compete with cheaper equivalents from Australia and the like.

Higher-quality offerings from the south come from the hills of Limoux, which, if you believe the locals, is the birthplace of sparkling wine production.

## wineries to watch
## rest of france

JAMES HERRICK

MAS DE DAUMAS GASSAC

MAS LA CHEVALIÈRE

ROBERT SKALLI

# italy

Given the amount of pride that the Italians take in their native grape varietals (indeed, their native anything), it's perhaps a bit of a surprise to find that Chardonnay has settled in here.

It's far more widespread than you might imagine, grown everywhere from the shimmering heat of Puglia in the south to the fragrant green of the Alpine foothills in the north. Although it is found as far south as Sicily, the grape is something of a rarity in the bottom half of Italy. In the north, however, it is widely planted and even officially sanctioned in some regions, playing an active part in DOC wines (see opposite).

Chardonnay in Italy generally gives the best results at altitude and, like in Burgundy, on chalky, alkaline soils. There are some particularly vibrant examples from the lower slopes of the Alps, near the Austrian border, and the hills of Piedmont.

For years Chardonnay used to be mistaken in Italy for Pinot Bianco, though how genuine the confusion was is open to question. Some have suggested that the authorities knew perfectly well what the grape in question was, but, proud Italians that they were, preferred not to give official sanction to a French grape varietal!

Either way, the grape has been popular in Italy since the mid-1970s—about as long as in Australia. And you'd be hard-pushed to block out its existence in the areas north and west of Venice, where it makes tens of thousands of bottles of straight Chardonnay as well as being mixed in with the local Garganega grape. These wines don't see much if any oak, and are designed to be drunk young and fresh.

But Chardonnay in Italy is typically versatile. As well as cheap 'n' cheerful wines from Friuli, it makes sparkling wine from Franciacorta, east of Milan, intense "passito" wines (where the grapes are left to shrivel), plus excellent and much pricier wines in places like Tuscany. Here the grape is treated like an unwanted foreign interloper by officialdom, and is banned from use in DOC wines. The supposedly inferior classification under which it has to be sold, however, doesn't appear to have affected its ability to command serious money. The version from Isole e Olena is one of the few in Italy that will age.

Many of these white so-called Supertuscans are planted in places that used to grow red Sangiovese for Chianti, but struggled to get it ripe and gave eminently forgettable wine as a result. Only the most one-eyed traditionalist would think that turning over some of these vineyards to a perfectly suitable, albeit non-native, white grape is a bad move.

THE DOC

The DOC (Denominazione di Origine Controllata) is Italy's equivalent of France's appellation system. To qualify for the DOC seal of approval, wines must come from within a certain region and be made with certain (usually traditional) grapes.

wineries to watch
italy

| | |
|---|---|
| CA' DEL BOSCO | PLANETA |
| GAJA | RUFFINO |
| ISOLE E OLENA | TIEFENBRUNNER |
| JERMANN | |

# spain and portugal

There is much debate in Spain at the moment about whether it's right or not that the country should use a non-native grape like Chardonnay.

Frankly, given the choice offered by most of Spain's indigenous grape varieties, it's a bit of a no-brainer. With the exception of Albariño in the far northwest and the aromatic Verdejo in Rueda, Spain's white grapes don't have a lot to recommend them, and Chardonnay should be welcomed with open arms.

As you'd expect, it is most widely found in the areas nearest the French border—in Somontano in the foothills of the Pyrenees and, increasingly, on the high plains and hills around Penedès in Catalonia, where the cooler sites help it give of its best.

It's even starting to find its way into the Spanish fizz, cava, after a lengthy stand-off between modernizers (who wanted Chardonnay permitted) and traditionalists (who thought anyone who used it should be burned at the stake for heresy). Whether you agree or not, the end results in terms of taste are encouraging, and it's likely that the grape's influence in the country's sparkling wine world is going to increase.

Arguably, however, the grape has settled in best in Navarra, where it's increasingly widely planted.

Although Navarra is Rioja's northeastern neighbor, it could hardly be more different in terms of attitude. While Rioja clings tenaciously to its traditions, Navarra is very open to new ideas.

So, while Chardonnay is banned from Spain's most famous wine region by all apart from a few daring experimenters, just over the border the Navarrans have shown a real interest in it. Not surprising, either, because the cool Atlantic-influenced weather in the north of the region can give a Chardonnay of no small finesse—particularly in the hands of masters like Chivite, who makes an excellent neo-Burgundian version.

It can be barrel-fermented (as in Burgundy) and proudly trumpeted on the label, like an Australian or California version. But in Navarra Chardonnay is sometimes also given a Spanish twist, when it's blended with the local Viura. Viura is an aromatic but fairly lightweight grape variety and, though not hugely exciting on its own, it combines well with Chardonnay. The latter adds a bit of depth and roundness, gaining some spritzy perfume from its Spanish counterpart. A happy marriage of modern and traditional; of local and foreign.

## wineries to watch
### spain

| | |
|---|---|
| RENE BARBIER | NEKEAS |
| CHIVITE | RAIMAT |
| ENATE | TORRES |

### PORTUGAL

Across the border in Portugal, Chardonnay has been much slower to take off. The Portuguese have dozens of weird and wonderful native grape varieties of their own and have generally not seen much point in embracing a grape that is already on show just about everywhere else in the world.

The only region to show any interest is the Alentejo, the hot, flat dustbowl southeast of Lisbon, which has shown an admirably open-minded attitude over the last decade, and become something of a commercial success story as a result.

Some examples are encouraging, but the grape won't be a major force any time soon—if ever.

## wineries to watch
### portugal

| | |
|---|---|
| ESPORÃO | QUINTA DAS PANCAS |

# rest of europe

Europe's wine regions
have traditions that
stretch back hundreds
—indeed thousands—
of years, and these
traditions for the most
part don't include
Chardonnay.

But so adaptable has the grape proved to different climates and soils, and so popular has it proved with the world's wine drinkers, that just about everywhere in Europe has some Chardonnay vines growing. And, significantly, plantings are on the up.

In places like Greece, it remains very much a minority interest, but in Central Europe it's gaining ground at quite a pace. Hungary, for instance, has always been big on white wine, and the country's wineries, fired up by the success their New World counterparts have had with the grape, have been planting Chardonnay enthusiastically.

The wines aren't really any better than good to competent yet, but let's not write them off. After all, Burgundy has taken hundreds of years to get where it is today.

Patience is needed in Bulgaria, too. While the country has a reputation for being able to knock out half-decent Cabernet Sauvignon for a bargain price, its track record with the world's favorite white grape is patchier. But the arrival of flying winemakers (peripatetic experts who zoom in, dispense wisdom, then zoom off again) from Chardonnay-friendly countries like Australia has helped, and we're starting to see some decent examples from a country that should make far better wines than it does.

Elsewhere in Europe, Germany is best known for being able to do great things with the majestic Riesling grape. But some of the country's warmer areas, like Baden and the Pfalz, have been experimenting, and have discovered a somewhat surprising affinity

wineries to watch

**austria**

VELICH

**bulgaria**

BLUERIDGE

VARNA

**england**

NYETIMBER

RIDGE VIEW

with Chardonnay. It's not likely ever to be anything other than a novelty here, but it does show just how versatile the grape can be.

Austria, to the south, is warmer and has rather more of the grape, particularly in the southern region of Styria. Down around the Slovenian border, Burgundy's finest manages to produce sharp, but not half-bad wines, even if it is doing it under the Austrian local name of Morillon.

There is no such obfuscation in what has to be Chardonnay's most northerly outpost. Believe it or not, Chardonnay is grown in cold, rainy Britain. It's not, I hasten to add, planted in any great numbers, nor is it used to make still wine. But a few dedicated souls have used it to make sparkling wines—and (even more amazingly) achieved extraordinarily good results. That's because Sussex (where it's planted) isn't any cooler than Champagne, the grape is mixed with its old partners in fizz, Pinot Noir and Pinot Meunier, and, perhaps most significantly of all, the same chalk ridge that runs through northeast France resurfaces across the south of England. No wonder the wines often compete favorably with their French counterparts in blind tastings.

When you talk about wine in the US, you're largely talking about

# california

California has by far the biggest area under vine and the most producers in the country. And when you're talking about white wine in California, Chardonnay is where it's at. It makes up half of all the state's white vines, and is the most planted grape, red or white, by quite a distance.

But this isn't purely a California success story; the grape has put down roots right across the country, from Washington State in the north down to near Los Angeles in the south, and from Sonoma's Pacific Coast to Long Island on the Atlantic.

So, given that there's so much of it, and it's so popular, why don't the country's Chardonnays attract the big price tags and glaring media exposure of its Cabernet Sauvignons?

There are probably three reasons. For a start, while there are many good California Cabernets that will age for more than ten years, no one has really managed to pull off the same trick with Chardonnay. Five years of aging, yes—but by their tenth birthday California Chardonnays are starting to run out of steam. And the longevity typified by great Burgundy—that a wine has the legs to develop and gain in complexity over many years—is the hallmark of a really fine wine.

This isn't purely a **California success story;** the grape has put down roots **right across the country,** from Sonoma's Pacific Coast to Long Island on the Atlantic.

The second point holding back the grape's development is, paradoxically, its extraordinary popularity on the home market. For thousands of American wine lovers, white wine **is** Chardonnay— and their favorite bottles are big, round, and soft. Nice big "mouthfeel" and not too much acidity. So those winemakers who want to produce more challenging wines need to have cojones of steel to go against the wishes of the market. It's hard to imagine a wine as steely as Chablis, for instance, ever being made in California.

Finally, there's the Napa Valley factor. By some distance, it's the best-known California wine-producing area. But it's famous for its Cabernets, not its Chardonnays. The grape is grown here (mostly in the cooler southern third of the valley), but it doesn't attract anything like the attention of its red counterpart. That's because most of Napa is too warm. And if it's good Chardonnay you're after, you need to look elsewhere.

BEYOND NAPA

Fortunately, you don't need to go too far to start looking. Carneros—one of the coolest sites in California—sits just at the bottom end of Napa Valley, butting up against the marshland to the north of the San Francisco Bay.

Wind is the key here. Boats in the bay can be heeled over on the blasts that roar in through the gap in the coastal range at San Francisco, and the first land they hit is Carneros.

Forget leisurely basking in the sun, a vine's life here is tough: thin poor soils, wispy fogs, and that wind make for scrawny, stunted-looking vines. But they also give long, slow ripening and a far cooler climate that works well for Chardonnay. Typically, Carneros Chardonnays are quite austere, with flavors from the crunchier end of the fruit spectrum: green apples, grapefruit, white peach, and sometimes a delicate floral note.

Carneros also runs across the bottom of Sonoma County, and it is here, rather than Napa, that northern California's best Chardonnays tend to be found. Like Napa, Sonoma has a lengthy history, but it's bigger and less glitzy than its neighbor, and there are more cool-climate, Chardonnay-friendly sites lurking among its folded hills and valleys.

Most of the good sites are in the cooler southern end of the region. But it's difficult to generalize too much, because the region's climate is so affected by the fogs that roll in off the Pacific, funneling down river valleys and dispersing quixotically wherever they feel like it.

What's definitely true is that there's a big difference in style between the warm Alexander Valley in the north, which gives rich, soft, tropical Chardonnays, and those of Russian River, Sonoma's best cool-climate site.

The Russian River Valley runs north–south almost the full length of Sonoma County before turning abruptly west to meet the sea. And it is down this opening that great thick banks of fog billow every evening, hanging around all night and dispersing grudgingly mid-morning.

It means that vines only get a brief blast of sunshine before the fog performs its cooling act again, giving, as in Carneros (but for different reasons), a slow ripening and wines with a fresh purity of flavor. Russian River wines have been described as a lemon drop wrapped in caramel oak, and they certainly offer flavors at the greener end of the scale: juicy citrus, apple, and pear are common.

Russian River might be Sonoma's best Chardonnay site, but Green Valley nearby (even cooler) is also on the up, while the new Sonoma Coast region, bordering the Pacific, could be the coolest of the lot. Vineyards here are above the fog line, but this close to the chilly Pacific there's a lot less heat, giving lean, minerally wines that cry out for shellfish.

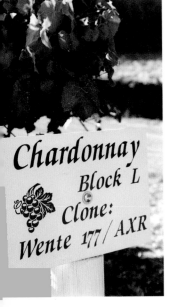

## SOUTH OF SAN FRANCISCO

You would think that the farther south of San Francisco you go, the hotter it would get and, therefore, the less conducive it would be to growing decent Chardonnay. But don't forget that the key influence on grape growing in California is not latitude, but the behavior of the sea breezes and fogs (see page 38).

There are some valleys south of Monterey that grow real cool-climate Chardonnay, where the fogs roll straight in off the sea and linger much the same way as they do in Sonoma's Russian River Valley. The result: cool, citrussy wines, while just 10 miles (15 km) inland it's as bare and parched as any desert.

In fact, two of California's best Chardonnay areas are 'way down south. The Edna Valley is around San Luis Obispo, and gives classy Chardonnays from limestone soils similar to those in Champagne. The ripening here is super-slow, and harvesting often isn't finished until November. Believe me, that's late.

Even farther south lies the Santa Maria Valley. Just north of Santa Barbara, it's closer to LA than it is to San Francisco, but it's proving itself to be something of a star with Chardonnay. Totally open to the sea, with no protecting mountain ranges, the Pacific air funnels in unchecked, making it decidedly cool; so much so that if growers get greedy and try to produce too many grapes, the vine can struggle to get them all ripe.

While the quality is impressive, the valley itself isn't much to write home about. Large, open, and featureless, the vineyards are enormous, split up into giant plots owned by the large wine companies. Romantic it ain't.

But without the intense heat of some other regions, and with minimal risk of either frost during spring or rain during harvest, Santa Maria is one of the most exciting regions for Chardonnay anywhere in California, giving delicate wines with a leafy, herby character.

### ELSEWHERE

Chardonnay is still going strong north of California as well. The Yakima Valley in Washington State is about on a level with Beaune. But there the similarity with Burgundy ends. East of the Cascades, the sun is more reliable and the rainfall almost non-existent, giving semi-desert conditions requiring irrigation. The Chardonnays here tend to be reliable rather than exciting.

Oregon is cooler, wetter, and climatically more unpredictable. It's gone long on Burgundy's red grape, Pinot Noir and, while there is Chardonnay as well, it's perhaps a surprise that there isn't more of it in this Pacific state.

Interestingly, Chardonnay is one of the few "classic" grapes to have migrated successfully across the US to the East Coast. There are quite a few vines in Virginia turning out acceptable Chardonnay, as are wineries on Long Island's North Fork, just a short hop from New York City.

### HOW THOSE CALIFORNIA FOGS WORK

Fog is the key to understanding a lot of California's climatic vagaries. With fierce sunlight and major hot afternoon temperatures, the state would be too hot to make decent wine at all—red or white—were it not for the proximity of the chilly Pacific.

The ocean acts like a giant cooling compress throughout the summer and, as hot air rises inland in the afternoon, cool air rushes in off the sea to take its place. Cool air hits warm land and the result is fog—and plenty of it, as anyone who's ever tried to photograph the Golden Gate Bridge knows.

This fog might not do much for tourists' photos, but it's great for grapes, since it cools things down and stops them from getting too ripe too quickly. And if you want to keep freshness in your white grapes, long slow ripening is the way to go, giving a good long "hang time."

DID YOU KNOW that American-produced "Chablis" is a cheap blend of undistinguished grape varieties and has nothing to do with Chardonnay?

DID YOU KNOW that a California wine labeled "Chardonnay" need contain only 75 percent of that grape?

## wineries to watch
## california

| | |
|---|---|
| AU BON CLIMAT | LANDMARK |
| BONNY DOON | MARIMAR TORRES |
| CHALONE | MOUNT VEEDER |
| CHATEAU ST. JEAN | ST. FRANCIS |
| CLOS DU BOIS | SAINTSBURY |
| FIRESTONE VINEYARD | SHAFER |
| FREEMARK ABBEY | STAG'S LEAP WINE CELLARS |
| GRGICH HILLS | TREFETHEN |

Chilean wine might be a relative newcomer to our dinner tables,
but don't let that fool you into thinking that the country has
only been making wine for 20 years.

The first European grapes arrived in the country as long ago as the 1860s. This was the time of the boom in the tin mines in the north of the country, and wealthy mining barons wanted to spend their money in a way that would prove they had breeding as well as pots of cash.

All things French were, at this time, terribly chic in Chile. And what could be trendier—or more self-indulgently elegant—than owning your own vineyard and producing a wine with your name on the label? Land was purchased, beautiful, elegant mansion houses were built—usually within a day's ride of the capital, Santiago—and vines (and winemakers) were brought over from France.

The result? So-called "international" grape varieties took root good and early—and winemakers reared on the vagaries of European weather systems soon discovered that Chile's is a

# chile and argentina

wineries to watch

chile

CONCHA Y TORO

ERRÁZURIZ

MICHEL LAROCHE/JORGE CODERCH

climate to die for. With sun guaranteed almost without a break from November through March, grapes are sure to ripen reliably and, significantly, growers are sure to have good conditions in which to harvest. This perfect climate, combined with the stacks of money that have gone into the wineries over the last 20 years, has led to plenty of attractive, well-made, and well-priced wines.

Where Chile has struggled until recently, however, has been in taking the step up and making genuinely characterful whites. Sure, the Chardonnays were pleasant, soft, and fruity, but they weren't tearing up too many trees. While the reds made great strides, Chardonnay stayed largely rooted to the spot.

The problem was that Chile's a great place to ripen fruit, but to make really good white wines you need more than just sun. Most of the whites were planted where it was too hot, so many top-end Chilean Chardonnays suffered from overripe flavors.

To compound the problem, winemakers in search of extra quality fermented the wines in expensive new oak barrels, like they do in Burgundy, adding still more sweet flavors. The result: gloopy, syrupy wines that were as in-your-face as an Andy Warhol painting, and about as pleasant to drink.

Then came the Casablanca Valley. This area roughly halfway between Santiago and the Pacific Coast is considerably cooler than the Central Valley, where most of the

grapes are grown. A fairly recent discovery, it has proved itself a great place for grapes that prefer less heat, like Sauvignon Blanc, (red) Pinot Noir, and Chardonnay. In fact, it's so cool that there can be problems with frost in springtime—a bit like in Burgundy.

The key to Casablanca—as with California to the north—is fog and breeze. These two elements mean that the grapes take longer to ripen, giving them more time to develop flavors. So, although Chilean whites often show tropical aromas, they tend to be pure, not cooked, and the grapes retain better acidity, which means more freshness.

Perhaps most heartening of all is the fact that the Coastal Range of mountains near to the Pacific in Chile is home to dozens of odd little valleys, facing in different directions. The overwhelming majority of them haven't been explored yet for grape growing, and any of them could turn out to be a superstar.

Winemakers are currently looking at the region of Leyda, which is reckoned to be even cooler than Casablanca. For brave winemakers who dare to dream, Chile offers real possibilities for Chardonnay beyond the everyday.

ARGENTINA

Argentina has been slower to make its mark than its neighbor across the Andes. For a start, it had an enormous and uncritical domestic market, which glugged back more or less whatever was put in front of it. Thus, there was no real incentive to mess around with expensive and temperamental foreign grape varieties. When that collapsed in the mid-1990s, producers realized they would have to change and invest in the sort of grapes that the rest of the world wanted to see made into wine. And obviously that meant Chardonnay.

The trouble is that Mendoza, where the vast majority of Argentina's grapes grow, is seriously hot: summer temperatures of 104°F (40°C) are normal, which doesn't do much for white wines.

And with the small matter of the Andes between the vineyards and the cooling Pacific, there's no sea influence to be had. To get the effects of a cooler climate, Argentina's winemakers have had to go not sideways toward water, but up.

That, combined with the steak-heavy diet, perhaps explains why Argentina is better known for its reds than its whites. But that's not to say that opportunities don't exist for white grapes. The higher you go, the cooler it is—and some of Argentina's best white-wine vineyards are very high. Tupungato, for instance, is at some 4,000 feet (1,200 meters). As a region, it offers the best potential for the country's Chardonnay.

### wineries to watch
### argentina

CATENA                    FINCA FLICHMAN

The higher you go, the cooler it is—and some of Argentina's best white-wine vineyards are very high.

There's no doubt about it. Aussie Chardonnay has been the white-wine success story of the last 20 years. So much so, in fact, that many wine drinkers have a hard time believing that the country grows any other white grapes at all.

# australia

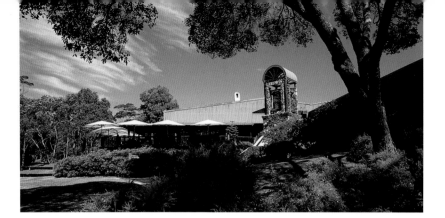

It does, of course, but it's easy to see where such a misconception comes from. After all, Chardonnay is Australia's most-planted white-wine grape by a country mile. There's four times as much of it as of its nearest rival, Semillon, and (get this) ten times as much as there is of the other great white heavyweight, Sauvignon Blanc.

Which makes it all the more amazing that 30 years ago you'd have had to search pretty hard to find any Chardonnay vines Down Under at all. They existed, but not in huge numbers and, hard though it is to believe now (given the ubiquity of Aussie Chardonnay), were often used in humble blends, or made wine labeled as "White Pinot."

The seeds of the Great Chardonnay Revolution began one evening in the late 1960s, when the irrepressible Murray Tyrrell hopped the fence of his neighbor's vineyard in the Hunter Valley and stole some Chardonnay cuttings. He grew the plants, harvested the crop, and, significantly, made it into a straight Chardonnay. The end result, Vat 47, hit the market in 1973. It showed just what Chardonnay was capable of in Australia, the public loved it, and before long everybody was at it.

Murray Tyrrell's benchmark effort is all the more remarkable given that the Hunter Valley derives as much of its popularity from its proximity to Sydney as it does from nature's bounty. With a subtropical climate that tends to dump rain on vines at harvest time and truculent clay soils, grape growing here is not a job for the faint-hearted. No surprise, then, that although the Hunter may have been where modern Australian Chardonnay started, other regions have since steamed on and left it behind.

If you've ever bought a bottle of cheap 'n' cheerful Aussie Chardie (as the winemakers affectionately call it), the chances are that it came from the Riverland. This is a vast, flat area of, essentially, desert, 100 miles (150 km) or so northeast of Adelaide. In the baking Aussie interior, the sun beats down day after day, rainfall is practically non-existent, and the soils are sandy, giving the plants minimal nutrients. As you can imagine, growing grapes in such an area poses a very different set of problems from those encountered by, say, your average Burgundian.

While the latter often has to fight to get his grapes ripe, the areas that supply the bulk of Australia's Chardonnays pose the opposite problem. With this much sun and heat, there's a real problem of grapes ripening too fast. An accelerated growing season can lead to grapes attaining "sugar ripeness" without ever really building up much flavor. The result: wine that's high in alcohol and low in taste. Australia still makes plenty of wine like this, but hardly any of it is exported, thank God. In super-hot areas, it's also easy to get unpleasant, cooked, overripe flavors. Many Australian Chardonnays of the 1980s and early 1990s had these kind of fat, canned-pineapple aromas, exacerbated by heavy-handed use of wood. The result was syrupy, sweet wines with all the finesse of a miner's pit-boot.

How things have changed. The last decade has seen leaner, more elegant Chardonnays come from even hot, big-volume regions like the Riverland; wines with pure, balanced fruit flavors that offer astonishing value for money. They're not exciting, but they're very gluggable.

Giving the vine a different haircut can expose or shield grape bunches from the sun.

How do they do it? The appliance of science. The Aussies have worked hard to understand how best to manipulate what nature has given them. They've done research into finding out how adding different amounts of water to vines at different times of year affects a grape's flavor. And they've looked into canopy management, which is essentially knowing how giving the vine a different haircut can expose or shield grape bunches from the sun—and what this does to the taste. It's complicated stuff, but they've made it work for them.

On top of that, winemakers can blend wines from pretty much all over the country to create their famous brands, an advantage denied their European counterparts. With millions of bottles resting on their palates, Aussie winemakers know all about stress. But with their impressive grasp of technological wizardry in the winery, no wonder that they and their viticultural colleagues are so sought after all around the world.

Not that all of Australia's wine is produced on such an industrial scale. The big, aggressively priced brands might be what have turned wine drinkers all over the world (and especially northern Europe) onto the delights of Chardonnay, but a whole host of smaller, higher-quality wine estates have come steaming in behind.

Arguments still persist about which are the best areas for producing genuine top-quality Chardonnay, partly because the forgiving nature of the grape has meant that it has done well virtually wherever it's been planted. But the search for top spot seems to come down to three areas.

The Adelaide Hills, as you might gather from the name, are close to Australia's wine capital Adelaide and, er, hilly... Like many Australian wine regions, it boomed in the 19th century, then died, before being revived almost single-handedly in the 1970s by Brian Croser, who founded Petaluma. The Adelaide Hills aren't far from the coast, and —at 1,300 feet (400 meters)—pretty high. As a result, for all that there's plenty of sun, winters can be cold and summers cool. The result is wonderfully structured, aromatic Chardonnays with fine, elegant acidity. They can be drunk young, but also age well.

As the Adelaide Hills are to Adelaide, so the Yarra Valley is to Melbourne. It's one of the oldest wine regions in the country, and home to a broad spread of excellent wines of all styles. Cool, misty, and undulating, it has a bewildering array of slopes and soils to choose from. Regions nearby make skeletal Chardonnays in the style of Chablis, or wines used as the base for sparklers. But the Yarra manages to get the grapes ripe enough to produce Chardonnays of real poise and elegance, but with plenty of fruit, too. The biggest problem in the region, in fact, is not natural at all, but the encroaching suburbs of Melbourne to the west.

Away over on the other side of the country, Margaret River has been making waves since its recovery in the 1970s, mostly, fittingly enough, at the hands of doctors who swapped their stethoscopes for a tractor. It's a region that gets huge amounts of sun and heat, both factors modified by the strong winds that hurtle in off the Indian Ocean, and the best wines go for big bucks.

All the three regions above produce, if you like, cool-climate wines with plenty of sun—an enviable combination. Other areas such as Padthaway and McLaren Vale produce hotter, richer, more tropical wines, while those of Tasmania are decidedly cooler.

The point is, though, that there isn't a typical Australian Chardonnay any more than there's a typical European one. This enormous country has driven the world's Chardonnay boom. And for that it deserves both our praise and our respect.

wineries to watch
australia

| | |
|---|---|
| CAPE MENTELLE | MOSS WOOD |
| CHAIN OF PONDS | MOUNT MARY |
| COLDSTREAM HILLS | NEPENTHE |
| CULLEN | PETALUMA |
| DE BORTOLI | PIPERS BROOK |
| DIAMOND VALLEY | TARRAWARRA |
| GIACONDA | TYRRELL'S |
| LEEUWIN ESTATE | YARRA RIDGE |
| LENSWOOD | YARRA YERING |

The forgiving nature of the grape has meant that it has done well virtually wherever it's been planted.

# new zealand

New Zealand is unusual in that it's the only New World country to have made its name with white wine. Even more unusually, its number one white grape is not Chardonnay, but the super-pungent Sauvignon Blanc.

Sauvignon might be New Zealand's signature grape varietal, but until fairly recently Chardonnay was the country's most-planted quality grape. It's still a good second behind its aromatic rival, way ahead of (red) Merlot, Cabernet Sauvignon, and Pinot Noir.

It's not hard to see why, either, because New Zealand is well suited to the grape. It's a country of two islands. The North Island is, broadly speaking,

fairly lush and tropical, while the South Island is cooler, particularly in the south. Between them, they offer myriad opportunities to growers to produce Chardonnay in pretty much any style they want.

Let's start in the North Island. Gisborne, on the east coast, is an area of incredible fertility and a warm, equable climate. For most grapes, it's too humid and the soil is too rich. But, provided growers control their yields, the ever-tolerant Chardonnay makes wines of roundness and generosity here.

Many Gisborne wines are used as padding, to provide a bit of richness and alcohol to slimmer, more structured wines from farther south. But some producers are battling the dampness and the vine's tendency to overproduce to make genuinely characterful wines here—and plenty claim that it's actually the best place in the country for the grape.

Hawke's Bay, farther south, is warm and sunny, too, but it's also drier and, significantly, the soils are poorer. All this means naturally lower yields, better concentration and, provided the weather behaves, ripe, round, tropical wines that rarely get overripe.

There is something of a battle at the moment over whether Gisborne or Hawke's Bay produces the best Chardonnays. One thing both have to contend with is frost. Since it's so warm, the vines tend to get a bit advanced in the North Island, and an early budder like Chardonnay will show signs of life even earlier than usual. A mild start to spring followed by a couple of sub-zero nights and, Bang!, half the year's crop is wiped out by frost damage.

Move 250 miles (400 km) across the Cook Strait and into the top tip of the South Island, however, and you're into a whole new scenario. This is Marlborough, stamping ground of Sauvignon Blanc and probably the country's best-known region.

It's a lot cooler. There's plenty of sun, but without the high temperatures (few red grapes here), which means a long, long growing season. Grapes can hang on the vines here until well into the fall, giving plenty of time for flavors to develop.

That's the theory, but it seems to work better in practice for Sauvignon Blanc than for Chardonnay. Good Chardonnays are made down here, but they are surprisingly few and far between, and most of the grape's wines are used for Kiwi sparkling wine.

New Zealand might not be as reliable as some of its New World counterparts with Chardonnay, but when it gets it right, the results are impressive.

## wineries to watch
## new zealand

| | |
|---|---|
| ESK VALLEY | SILENI |
| HUNTER'S | VILLA MARIA |

# south africa

Given that the world's greatest expressions of Chardonnay come from the cool surroundings of Burgundy, you might wonder whether it's possible to produce good expressions of the grape from somewhere like Africa, which prompts images of desert, savanna, and skeletons bleached in the sun.

Well, it is—and the South Africans are proving it. To be honest, Cape Province, where the country's wines are made, is not quite as hot as you might imagine. Sure, it gets a good deal of sun, and by the middle of February, temperatures can be brutal— but the Chardonnay tends to have been picked by then, and there are mitigating factors, too.

To start with, there's the wind. Whether the winds are from the southeast or the southwest, a place like Stellenbosch will feel them. And a cooling wind can make a real difference to grapes. Then there's the altitude. The higher you go, the cooler it is—and the tip of South Africa has plenty of mountains. Grow grapes at altitude (as they do in

Argentina, for instance), and the flavor profiles are very different, with temperatures dropping hugely at night—helping to preserve the grapes' acidity.

In any case, the Cape is too big to generalize about. The region of Elgin, surrounded by high mountains, is cool, lush, and drizzly. Chardonnay from here can be elegantly citrous, with lemon and even grapefruit flavors. Move closer to the Indian Ocean in Walker Bay, and you find wines with a finesse that can border on the Burgundian.

Stellenbosch, South Africa's best-known wine region, might not generally go a bundle on whites, but there are producers here making very good Chardonnays—usually from sites that get a little less sun or sit in a wind-trap. As one winemaker puts it, "Each valley is a Napa Valley on its own." With this many different soils, exposures, and microclimates, one should be wary of the broad-brush approach to Stellenbosch. While some areas make huge, blockbuster reds, there are others that produce delicate, minerally whites, and others making bigger, full-bodied, fruit-driven examples.

Nevertheless, the region that is becoming the country's center of Chardonnay production is Robertson. This inland area is generally shielded from both wind and rain—and it's hot and exceptionally arid. Without irrigation, nothing would grow here at all, but with a little water the whole place springs into life. Gardens burst with exotic tropical plants, and vines greedily suck up the relentless sunshine.

Left to its own devices, Chardonnay here will be bland and characterless—plenty of ripeness, but not a great deal of flavor. So the wineries work hard at, if you like, cooling things down. The farther away you get from the baking heat of the ground, the cooler it is. So vines are trained higher, while plants are pruned to keep the grapes partly hidden from the sun.

It's worth it, because Robertson has that priceless commodity for Chardonnay: limestone-rich soils. Gazillions of years ago, the area was a huge lake, whose floor became caked in yards of dead sea creatures. Their calcified remains have given rise to a large lime factory—and the burgeoning center of South African Chardonnay production.

## wineries to watch
## south africa

| | |
|---|---|
| BOUCHARD-FINLAYSON | JORDAN |
| DE WETSHOF | THELEMA |
| GLEN CARLOU | VERGELEGEN |
| HAMILTON RUSSELL | WARWICK ESTATE |

So, the professionals of the wine world have done their bit. The growers have brought the grapes to ripeness; the winemakers have turned the crop into wine; and retailers have got it onto their shelves. Now you've bought it, and the responsibility turns over to you.

After all, it's still possible for a few dodgy decisions at your end to ruin the best efforts of even the most conscientious grower. Chardonnay served five years past its peak, at room temperature, in a tiny glass and with a whopping steak is unlikely to be a wine to savor.

Just how should you get the most out of your glass of the world's most popular white grape, then? Read on to find out.

# ENJOYING

The whole idea of learning how to taste might seem a bit ridiculous. I mean, surely you just chuck the wine in your mouth, check the flavors, and swallow, right?

# how to taste

Well, you can do that, of course. But if you want to get the most out of what you're drinking, you'll want to take the art of tasting one step further. It's not complicated or pretentious, but a bit of extra effort will make a big difference to your overall enjoyment.

### THE BASICS

Before you even pour the wine, there are a couple of things you want to get right. First, glasses. As a general rule of thumb, the bigger the better, since you can pour a decent measure of wine and still swirl it around, which releases the aromas. That's why those tiny glasses so beloved of cheap restaurants are a total waste of time.

Second, temperature. White wine needs to be chilled—but not too cold. If a bottle is too chilly, it will kill many of the aromas and you might as well be drinking water. So if you have a particularly ferocious fridge, you'll probably want to take the bottle out 15 minutes beforehand to get it to the right temperature.

If you want specifics, 50°F (10°C) is about right. But think cool rather than cold and, especially for good wine, err on the side of being too warm.

## IN THE EYE

So, you've poured the wine—about a third of a glass is good. Take a look at the color. If it's a deep, burnished gold, it's showing signs of maturity; if it's more lemony, it's probably still youthful and zingy. If it's hazy, it's faulty and should be taken back to where you bought it.

## ON THE NOSE

After you've swirled the wine around a bit, stick your nose in the glass and take a good deep breath. It shouldn't really smell of wine, but fruit flavors. For Chardonnay, they could be anything from grapefruit, lemons, and apples through to pears, pineapples, and even nectarines and mangoes. Burgundies can be more savory: nutty and minerally. Aromas of vanilla, toast, or spices are the result of time the wine has spent in wooden barrels; creamier notes come from time spent on the lees.

Tasting is most fun in a group, when everyone throws in their own suggestions, but the key point is that there are no right and wrong answers. Tasting is highly subjective, so if you think a wine smells like grilled chicken drumsticks, say so!

## IN THE MOUTH

Take a mouthful and slosh it around. Check the "mouthfeel" (generous? austere? full-bodied? lean?) and structure, which for Chardonnay means acidity.

You feel acidity down the sides of your mouth—try sucking a lemon if you want to see what it's like in extremis. White wines need acidity to give them freshness and to help them age. Does the wine have a little or a lot? Too much or not enough?

Finally, the experimenting done, draw a few conclusions. Do you like it? Would you buy it again? Do you think it would improve with age or not?

The majority of Chardonnays on the market nowadays are designed to be drunk young, which suits our modern lifestyle.

# storing and serving

As one California winemaker wryly observed to me, "Most wine drinkers today age a wine for 15 minutes on the car seat on the way back from the store."

While such impatience might give you problems with red wines, for modern white wines it's no big deal. It certainly isn't for cheaper Chardonnays—and most New World offerings don't improve with significant aging. Having said that, there are some wines—generally more expensive bottles, specifically those from Burgundy—that will definitely improve with time. And, even if you're planning to drink a wine six months down the line, you'll want to keep it in the best conditions possible. Store a wine above a radiator for even a few weeks, and the heat will affect the flavor.

Cellars, obviously, are the ideal, since they are cool, dark, and at a consistent temperature. But should you not be lucky enough to have access to one, the key factors to look for are darkness and constancy of temperature. It's better to keep your wines somewhere that's dark and a bit warmer than the ideal, but steady (under the stairs, perhaps), than somewhere the temperature fluctuates from ideal to too hot (for example, the garage). And definitely keep them out of direct light!

Specifics about when to drink a wine are tricky, since they depend on the philosophy of the winemaker, the character of the vintage—and the kind of flavors that you like to see in your wines.

If you drink a Chardonnay young, it will generally taste fruitier and fresher—and the vast majority of Chardonnays will never get any better than this. But drinking truly fine Burgundies or Chablis too young is a real opportunity missed. With time, they acquire extraordinary depth and complexity that go way beyond fruit flavors. Good ones will easily last ten years or more, while even average examples from a decent vintage (and top-end New World Chardonnays) will improve after five years.

There are no hard and fast rules here, though. If you can, buy several bottles (or a case, if your budget will take it) of a wine that you're interested in aging, and try them at different times. That way, you're bound to get one at its peak, and seeing how the wines develop can be fascinating.

Specifics about when to drink a wine are tricky, since they depend on the philosophy of the winemaker, the character of the vintage—and the kind of flavors that you like to see in your wines.

# matching
## chardonnay and food

Part of Chardonnay's success lies in its full-bodied nature. It's a bigger, rounder wine than any of its white counterparts, and this gives it something of a headstart when it comes to food matching.

Sauvignon Blanc, for instance, is a seafood wine par excellence, but it's hard to imagine it going well with pork or chicken. Chardonnay, however, is versatile enough to do both.

Generally speaking, Chardonnays from cooler sites (like Casablanca, Chablis, Carneros) have "green" flavors—citrus fruit, apples, grapefruit, and lemons, with crunchy acidity—that make them good with lighter dishes such as fish, seafood, salads, and so on. Those from warmer areas (Rapel, Napa, Riverland) show more tropical fruit characteristics, which need something a bit more substantial, like baked chicken, turkey, or pork. Great Burgundies go with more or less anything— one of the reasons they're so well thought of.

But regional characteristics alone aren't the full story. As mentioned earlier, Chardonnay is the ultimate winemaker's grape, and the way in which it is handled in the winery has a huge impact on the final flavor.

In fact, probably as important as where the wine is grown is how it is dealt with after picking, particularly the amount of time it spends aging or fermenting in oak barrels. Big toasty oak flavors in a wine, for instance, will override delicate food, but be perfectly at home with grilled or broiled pork or chicken. Look on the back label for any information to help you make an informed choice.

In a really good Chardonnay, the wood should be so well integrated that you don't really notice it as a stand-out flavor component—and mercifully we're starting to see such restraint more and more after the oak-crazy days of the 1990s.

Chardonnay is a bigger, rounder wine than any of its white counterparts, and this gives it something of a headstart when it comes to food matching.

TWO FINAL TIPS

1. If you ever serve a really great wine, keep the food simple and let the wine strut its stuff unimpeded.

2. Don't worry too much about getting it wrong. Fear of failure is the biggest paralyzing factor that stops people from experimenting in wine. So go with your instincts, go with what you like, and keep drinking around!

All photographs by Alan Williams
unless otherwise stated.

Key: ph=photographer, a=above, b=below, r=right, l=left, c=center.

Page 4 ph Francesca Yorke; 15l courtesy of Louis Jadot; 15r ph Francesca Yorke; 18, 19, & 22 courtesy of Louis Jadot; 23 & 24 ph Peter Cassidy; 26 & 27 © ph Alan Williams; 39 ph Francesca Yorke; 40, 41, 42l, & 42r © Viña Errazuriz; 42c © Concha y Toro; 43 © Familia Zuccardi; 50 & 51 © Esk Valley Estates; 52 ph Alain Proust, commissioned by Graham Beck Wines; 55l ph Francesca Yorke; 55r ph Nicky Dowey; 56, 57, & 59b ph Francesca Yorke; 60 ph Martin Brigdale; 61 & 64 ph Francesca Yorke.

The publisher would like to thank R&R Teamwork, Hatch Mansfield, Mandarin Communications, and Emma Wellings PR for providing pictures from the following wine producers:
Concha y Toro, Chile
Viña Errazuriz, Chile
Familia Zuccardi, Chile
Louis Jadot, France
Esk Valley Estates, New Zealand
Graham Beck Wines, South Africa

# picture credits

# index

Thanks to my parents for introducing me to wine at an early age, to my lovely wife, Bola, who has borne my vinous ramblings down the years with great good humor, and to my daughter Rebecca who makes it all worthwhile.

# acknowledgments